ACTION SPORTS
EQUESTRIAN SPORTS

Joe Herran and Ron Thomas

CHELSEA HOUSE
PUBLISHERS
A Haights Cross Communications Company
Philadelphia

Chelsea House Publishers
1974 Sproul Road, Suite 400
Broomall, PA 19008-0914

The Chelsea House world wide web address is www.chelseahouse.com

Library of Congress Cataloging-in-Publication Data

Herran, Joe.
    Equestrian sports / Joe Herran and Ron Thomas.
    p. cm. — (Action sports)

    Summary: Surveys the history, equipment, techniques, and safety aspects of equestrian sports, including jumping, dressage, vaulting, and reining, plus short biographies of top riders and a time line.

    ISBN 0-7910-7533-8
    1. Horse sports—Juvenile literature. [1. Horse sports. 2. Horsemanship.] I. Thomas, Ron, 1947–
    II. Title. III. Series.
    SF294.23.H37 2004
    798.2—dc21

                                                                          2003001179

First published in 2003 by
MACMILLAN EDUCATION AUSTRALIA PTY LTD
627 Chapel Street, South Yarra, Australia, 3141

Associated companies and representatives throughout the world.

Edited by Renée Otmar, Otmar Miller Consultancy Pty Ltd, Melbourne
Text and cover design by Karen Young
Page layout by Raul Diche
Photo research by Legend Images

Printed in China

Acknowledgements
The author and the publisher are grateful to the following for permission to reproduce copyright materials:

Cover photograph: Kerry Millikin of the USA clears a fence in the showjumping section of the 50th Badminton Horse Trials, May 9, 1999, courtesy of Reuters.

AP/Wide World Photos, p. 27 (left); Australian Picture Library/Corbis, pp. 6, 30; Kate Drinnan, pp. 8, 9, 11, 13, 14, 15, 16–17, 18, 19, 20, 24; Getty Images, pp. 4, 28; Jiri Lochman/Lochman Transparencies, p. 12; Reuters, pp. 5, 7, 21, 22, 23, 25, 26, 27 (right), 29.

While every care has been taken to trace and acknowledge copyright, the publisher tenders their apologies for any accidental infringement where copyright has proved untraceable. Where the attempt has been unsuccessful, the publisher welcomes information that would redress the situation.

CONTENTS

INTRODUCTION

In this book you will read about:

- equestrian horses and gear
- safety measures used to keep riders safe
- how to take care of a horse
- some basic skills, tricks and techniques
- equestrian competitions
- some top equestrians in competition today
- the history of equestrian competition from the 1800s.

In the beginning

People have been taming horses since prehistoric times. They have used horses as a means of transportation and to help on farms. Since the invention of machines, the power and agility of the horse have been used by people for pleasure riding and in sporting competitions.

Equestrian sports developed during the late 1800s. By 1900, equestrian events were part of the Olympic Games. These first Olympic horse-riding events, held in Paris, France, were open only to army officers. For the Stockholm Olympics of 1912, Count Clarence von Rosen prepared a full program of equestrian events. These events have continued on the Olympic program to this day. In 1921, the Fédération Equestre Internationale (FEI) was formed to regulate international competitions and the events at the Olympics.

Equestrian sports today

Today, equestrian events take place in countries around the world, as events at local shows and riding clubs, as national competitions and at large international events such as the Olympic Games. Different breeds of horse are used for different purposes depending on the horse's abilities and **temperament**.

 **Warning** This is not a how-to book for aspiring equestrians. It is intended as an introduction to the exciting world of equestrian sports, and a look at where the sport has come from and where it is heading.

WHAT ARE EQUESTRIAN SPORTS?

The word "equestrian" comes from the Latin word *equestri*, meaning "of a horseman." Although horses are involved in many sports, including horse racing and polo, the word "equestrian" is used only for those sports regulated by the FEI.

The FEI regulates the equestrian sports of:

- **jumping**
- **dressage**
- **eventing**
- **driving**
- **endurance**
- **vaulting**
- **reining**.

Code of conduct

The FEI has developed a "Code of Conduct" for equestrian events. The Code explains how riders should behave and how they should treat and look after their horses. The first rules of the Code state that:

- in all equestrian sports, the horse must be considered before anything else
- the well-being of the horse shall be above the demands of breeders, trainers, riders, owners, dealers, organizers, sponsors or officials
- men and women are considered equal in competition.

The FEI regulates all equestrian sports, including dressage.

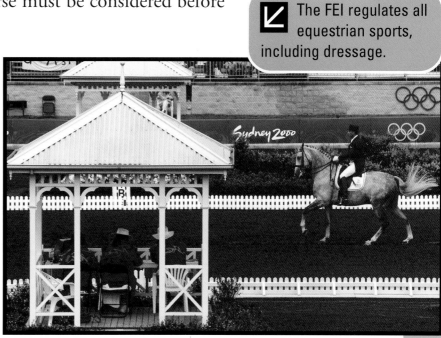

5

THE HORSE

Horse breeds

There are more than 150 different breeds of horses and ponies in the world. Horse breeds used in equestrian events include the Arab, Anglo-Arab, Thoroughbred, the Trakehner and the Holstein. The Anglo-Arab is a cross between an Arab and the fastest breed of horse, the Thoroughbred. Horses are chosen for the different events depending on their build, strength, stamina and temperament. For example, the Holstein is a strong, intelligent and bold breed, which makes it an ideal choice for dressage and show-jumping events.

The Arab is the oldest of all horse breeds. Its fine features and gracefulness, together with its gentle temperament, make it a popular equestrian horse.

Conformation

The overall shape and size of all the parts of a horse is known as the conformation. A rider should know the parts of the horse to be able to choose the right horse and to look after it properly.

Colors and markings

Horses and ponies come in different colors and have different markings:

- bay horses are reddish-brown with black tails and manes
- palominos have a golden-colored coat with a paler, sometimes white, mane and tail
- duns have a light, sandy-colored coat with a black mane and tail.
  There are also gray, black, chestnut and piebald horses, which have coats covered in large patches of black and white.

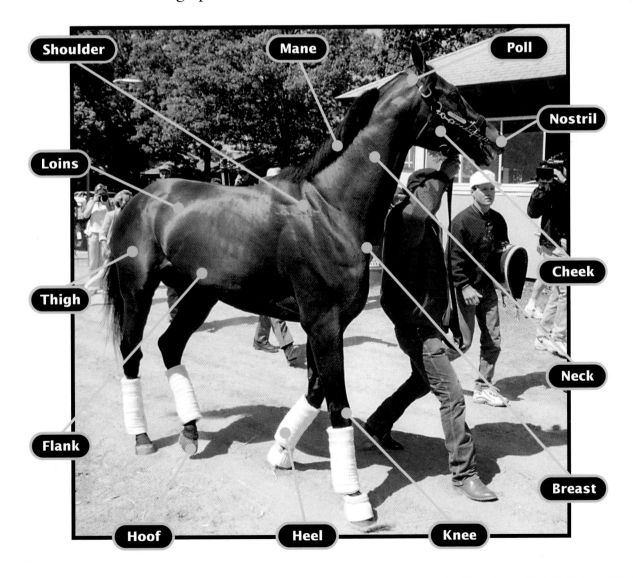

EQUESTRIAN GEAR

Tack

Tack is the gear that the horse wears when it is being ridden.

The saddle

The general-purpose **saddle** is the most widely used saddle. Saddles come in different sizes and shapes for special kinds of riding, such as dressage, jumping and racing. Almost all saddles are built on a solid frame called a tree, which once was always made of wood. Today, laminated wood, fiberglass and plastic are used to make the tree. Saddles are worn on a clean, smooth cloth called a saddle cloth. The saddle cloth absorbs the horse's sweat and stops the saddle from rubbing the horse's back.

Pommel

Seat

Girth

Stirrup

ACTION FACT

Some pony saddles for young children who are learning to ride are designed with a safety handle or a hand support for extra grip.

A saddle must be comfortable for both the rider and the horse.

Girth

The girth is a padded strap used to keep the saddle in place on the horse's back. It is attached to one side of the saddle and is passed under the horse and fastened at the other side of the saddle.

Stirrups

Stirrups, also known as irons, hang from the saddle on leathers. Stirrups give riders a place to put their feet. They are almost always made of extremely strong stainless steel, so that they will not rust. To be the right length, the bottom of each stirrup rests on or just above the rider's ankle bone. Stirrup irons should be wide enough to allow about a half inch (1.5 centimeters) on either side of the rider's foot so that the foot does not get caught in it.

Bridle and bit

The bridle is worn on the horse's head. It is used by the rider to help control the horse. Bridles are usually made of leather. The bit, made of steel or rubber, is the part of the bridle that fits inside the horse's mouth. The **reins** are attached to the bit.

↗ A rider fastens the girth to keep the saddle in place.

Bridle

Bit

Reins

↗ The bridle is worn over the horse's head, the bit fits into the horse's mouth, and the reins are attached to the bit.

Rider's clothing

Riders wear special clothes to keep them safe and comfortable when riding in equestrian events. Jackets and sweaters with long sleeves are worn to keep the rider warm in cold weather. Jackets should be kept fastened because a flapping jacket may frighten the horse.

Hard hat

All riders must wear a hard riding hat, also called a crash hat or helmet. A hard hat has a chinstrap to hold the hat in place. Hard hats come in various shapes but are lightweight and must conform to safety standards. Covers, called silks, can be worn over some kinds of riding hats.

Riding boots

Riding boots made of leather or rubber are designed to protect the rider's legs and ankles in the event of an accident. They also prevent the rider's feet from sliding through the stirrup irons and from getting caught in the irons if the rider falls off the horse. Boots are either long or short. Long boots are worn for most forms of competitive riding.

Gloves

Gloves are worn to protect the rider's hands from blisters and to stop the reins from slipping through the fingers. Gloves often have a special non-slip padding on the palms.

Trousers

Riders wear jodhpurs or special riding pants made of a cotton and lycra blend. These riding trousers are close-fitting and stretchy and are designed to keep the rider comfortable. Trousers that are too thick will chafe against the skin. Trousers that are too thin will wear through very quickly.

Chaps

Chaps are shaped leggings made from leather, suede or waterproof material. Chaps help protect the rider's calf from rubbing against the stirrup leather. Chaps also keep the rider warm in cold weather.

Body protector

A body protector is a padded vest made of lightweight material. It is used to cushion the rider's torso and shoulders in a fall. A body protector can be worn either over or under the rider's shirt or sweater.

Chinstrap

Hard hats

Jacket

Body protector

Gloves

Trousers or jodhpurs

Chaps

Riding boots

11

EQUESTRIAN SAFETY

Riding can be a dangerous sport. In order to stay safe, a rider always:

- checks that the horse's tack is fitted correctly and is in good condition
- wears proper protective gear, including gloves, a hard hat, boots and body protector
- makes sure the chinstrap is fastened correctly when on the horse
- replaces a hat that has been damaged
- wears correct footwear

- has the correct stirrup size, a little more than 1 inch (3 centimeters) wider than the boot
- avoids riding on roads with poor visibility or after dark
- rides with the coat fastened; a flapping coat may frighten the horse
- ties up long hair to keep it out of the eyes, to stop it flying about and frightening the horse in windy weather, and to stop it from becoming tangled up in the riding tack
- wears a coat or sweater while mounted in cold weather
- wears soft contact lenses if her eyesight is poor
- uses hand signals to warn other road users where they are going
- lets someone know where he is going and when he expects to return when riding in the country.

It is safer to ride in a group than to ride alone.

Rider fitness

To be able to enjoy equestrian sports, a rider should be physically fit. This means being able to ride without becoming short of breath and being able to maintain a relaxed position in the saddle. Aerobic exercise such as jogging, cycling or running will improve a rider's fitness.

Warming up and keeping fit

Gentle stretching, jogging or jumping will warm up and loosen muscles before taking to the saddle. Warm, loose muscles work better and are less likely to cramp. Some exercises to stretch and relax muscles can be performed on the ground or while mounted on the horse.

- To loosen the thigh muscles, the rider grabs the right ankle with the right hand and lifts the foot up and behind. Then the stretch is repeated with the left ankle and hand.
- To strengthen the upper body, the rider raises both arms to shoulder height and twists the body from right to left.
- To relax and strengthen the shoulders, the rider rotates the arms backwards and forwards in a circling movement.

↗ A rider who warms up correctly will enjoy relaxed and comfortable riding.

CARING FOR THE HORSE

A healthy horse should be alert, with its eyes clear and wide open, ears pricking backwards and forwards. The horse's coat should be smooth and shiny. The horse should stand evenly on all four feet.

A rider caring properly for the horse:

- does not give a horse a long drink when it is hot and sweating, because this could make the horse ill
- rubs the horse down vigorously with a towel after a hot ride, before putting it back in the paddock or stable
- walks the horse for about half a mile (1 kilometer) to cool it down after a hard ride
- does not ride the horse immediately after it has eaten a meal, as this could make the horse ill
- makes sure that the horse has enough fresh food at all times
- feeds the horse from clean containers
- gives the horse fresh drinking water every day
- does not leave the horse standing for a long period of time in a muddy or wet spot
- is careful to see that the horse does not eat poisonous or harmful plants or weeds such as rhubarb, privet, oleander or rhododendron.

A farrier is a blacksmith who puts the shoes on a horse.

Grooming

Grooming is an important part of looking after a horse. It helps the horse's skin produce oils that maintain the coat and keep it in good condition. Grooming massages the horse and helps blood circulation. Grooming also gives the rider a chance to check the horse for any scratches and other injuries to the skin.

To protect the welfare of horses in competition, the FEI lists things that must be done to care for horses.

- Only horses of certain ages may compete in some competitions; for example, event horses must be at least 4 years old before they may compete in one-day events.
- Competition horses must have an up-to-date vaccination certificate.
- Competitors have a responsibility for the welfare of their own horse as well as the other horses in the competition. They must not bring a horse with a contagious disease to a competition.

Hard body brush to remove dirt from the horse's coat

Rubber curry comb to rub and clean the horse

Hoof pick and brush to clean the horse's hooves

Mane and tail combs to untangle the mane and tail

Soft body brush to remove smaller pieces of dirt from the coat

SOME HORSE-GROOMING EQUIPMENT

SKILLS, TRICKS AND
TECHNIQUES

The basics

Mounting

Mounting is done in several steps. The rider checks that the girth is tight and the stirrup irons are down. The rider mounts from the "near" or left side of the horse. The rider's left shoulder is near the horse's shoulder and the rider faces the horse's tail. The rider holds the reins firmly in the left hand together with a handful of mane to prevent the reins pulling on the horse's mouth. Holding the stirrup in the right hand, the rider turns the stirrup clockwise, places the left foot in the stirrup and presses down with the toe. With the right hand the rider takes hold of the **pommel**, springs up on the left leg and swings the right leg over the horse to land lightly in the saddle. The right foot is then placed in the stirrup.

Adjusting the tack

Once mounted on the horse, the rider must check and tighten the girth to make sure the saddle is sitting properly and securely on the horse. Then the stirrups are checked and adjusted so that the bottom of each stirrup rests on or just above the rider's ankle bone.

Dismounting

Dismounting a horse is the reverse of mounting. The rider takes the reins and a handful of mane in the left hand while holding the pommel with the right hand. The rider stands up in the stirrups, swings the right leg up, over and behind the saddle before taking the left foot out of the stirrup and dropping to the ground with the knees bent to absorb impact.

ACTION FACT

Mounting the horse from the left side dates from times when horses were used in battle. Riders mounted on the left so that their swords would not pierce the horse.

Mounting and dismounting a horse should be done smoothly to avoid frightening the horse.

Sitting in position

Sitting correctly in the saddle helps the rider to control the horse.

- The rider's head is held high, the chin is up, and the rider looks ahead.
- The rider sits up tall with a straight back.
- The arms are slightly bent and relaxed, elbows are close to the sides.
- The balls of the feet are on the stirrups, heels are down and toes point up and toward the horse.
- The rider holds the reins across the palm and between the thumb and the first finger of each hand.
- The hands are relaxed and ready to be moved backward and forward with the movement of the horse's head and neck.
- The rider sits well down in the center and on the lowest part of the saddle.
- The knees and thighs are close to the saddle.

> ◣ A rider's position on a horse is like standing with the knees bent. It is not like sitting in a chair!

Beyond the basics

Using natural and artificial aids

A rider communicates with the horse using the legs, hands, seat and voice. These signals are called natural aids. Other aids, known as artificial aids, include a riding whip, or **crop**, and spurs that are used to signal to the horse. Artificial aids are not used to punish the horse.

Walking forward

To signal the horse to move forward, the rider takes hold of the reins so that the horse feels contact between its mouth and the rider's hands. Using the legs, the rider applies firm, gentle pressure to the horse's sides, behind the girth. As the horse starts to move forward, the rider relaxes the legs. The horse nods its head as it walks and the rider relaxes the arms to allow the hands to move forward and back in rhythm with the horse's nodding head.

Stopping

To stop the horse, the rider sits well down in the saddle with a straight back and squeezes gently with the legs. The hands pull back on the reins. The horse will feel the resistance to its forward movement and will stop. As soon as the horse has stopped, the rider relaxes the hands, back and legs.

The rider signals what she wants the horse to do, using the reins and her legs. These signals are called aids.

Turning

To turn to the right, the rider pulls back on the right rein, loosens the left rein slightly and uses the legs to move the horse forward. The left leg is brought back to keep the horse moving while pressure is applied to the horse's right side. The horse bends gently around the rider's right leg while the left leg keeps the horse's hindquarters from swinging outward. To turn left, the same aids are used but in the opposite direction; that is, the left rein and right leg are moved back.

Gaits and transitions

Most horses move in four different ways, or gaits. The four main gaits are the walk, the trot, the canter and the gallop. To get a horse to move faster, the rider squeezes harder with the legs and relaxes pressure on the reins. When a horse changes from one gait to another, the movement is called a transition.

- **The walk**
  This is the slowest gait. The horse places its hooves on the ground, one hoof after the other. There are four beats to every stride.

- **The trot**
  This is a faster gait. It has two beats to every stride. The horse springs from one pair of diagonal legs to the other. To make the horse trot, the rider squeezes with the lower legs, gently but more firmly than for making the horse walk. A gentle kick may sometimes be required. For a comfortable ride, the rider posts, or moves up and down in the saddle, in rhythm with the horse's movement.

- **The canter**
  This is a fast, smooth gait. The horse places one leg, then two together and then the remaining leg to make three beats to every stride. The horse's head bobs slightly while cantering so the rider relaxes the reins and lets the hands move forward and back in rhythm with the horse's bobbing head.

- **The gallop**
  This is the fastest gait, with four beats to every stride. Each foot makes a beat, followed by a moment of silence when all four feet are off the ground.

↗ The canter is one of the four gaits in which a horse moves.

Jumping

As horse and rider approach a fence, the rider sits quietly to allow the horse to size up the height and position of the fence. The rider leans forward in the saddle and slides the hands forward to give the horse a longer rein so that it can stretch its head. The rider's head is up and the rider is looking between the horse's ears as the rider guides the horse firmly toward the center of the jump. The rider urges the horse on to make the jump by squeezing the horse with his legs. The horse raises its head and takes off into the air, using the power of its hind legs. The rider holds on to a handful of mane for balance, and avoids pulling back on the reins. In the air above the fence, the horse tucks up its legs and rounds its back. This position is called **bascule**. As the horse lands, the rider sits up straight and guides the horse away from the fence in a straight line.

Horses should be at least 4 years old before they jump.

↘ ACTION FACT

In some jumping events, a wall can be more than 6.5 feet (2 meters) high.

↗ The rider leans forward in the saddle and holds onto the mane for balance as the horse jumps.

IN COMPETITION

The FEI is in charge of all international equestrian competitions. It sets the rules of competition for dressage, show jumping, carriage driving, eventing, vaulting and endurance riding. The FEI also controls and approves the equestrian program for the Olympic Games.

Equestrian events at the Olympic Games

The first Olympic equestrian events were held at the Paris Olympic Games of 1900. Only male military officers were allowed to compete. There were three events:

- high jumping
- long jumping
- prize jumping.

Olympic equestrian events were discontinued in 1904 and 1908, but were re-introduced at the Stockholm Games in 1912. Three new events were added at these Games: dressage, show jumping and the three-day event. Competition was still open only to male military officers. In 1952, at the Helsinki Games, equestrian events were open to both male and female competitors.

In equestrian competition today, men and women compete in the same events. An Olympic equestrian program consists of individual and team events. The individual events are the dressage and show jumping. The three-day team event also includes dressage and show jumping, as well as an endurance event.

◸ Olympic equestrian riders compete as part of a team.

Dressage

"Dressage" is a French word derived from *dresser*, which means "to teach." Dressage began as a training exercise for horses used in military operations. There are easier dressage tests at local club and international competitions, but in Olympic competition the horse and rider perform two tests, the Grand Prix and the Grand Prix Special. These difficult tests show how well the horse has been trained to perform a series of 36 movements. One of these movements, the piaffe, is a slow trot on the spot to test balance, strength and control. A second movement, the pirouette, in which the horse turns a complete circle on the spot and at a canter, tests the horse's balance and suppleness. A third test is the freestyle, which has horse and rider performing movements to music.

Judges award points for how well the movements are done (technical skill) and for how gracefully and rhythmically the movements are performed (artistic performance).

In dressage competition, the rider uses small and invisible commands so that the horse seems to be performing on its own.

Show jumping

In show-jumping events, horse and rider must travel a set course and jump 12 to 15 obstacles and a water jump. Twisting and turning sharply, rider and horse must complete the course in a set time. Points are deducted if an obstacle is knocked down, if a horse fails to jump an obstacle or if the time limit is exceeded. There are two show-jumping events in the Olympics, one for teams of four riders and another for individual riders.

↗ Show jumping has developed from the high-jumping and long-jumping competitions that were first included in the Olympics in 1900.

Three-day event

The three-day event consists of dressage, show jumping and endurance. There is a three-day event for individual riders and a three-day event for teams of four riders. Dressage and show jumping follow the same rules as regular dressage and show-jumping events. The endurance part of the event consists of four sections:

- two road-and-track sections, in which the horse may walk, trot and canter along a marked route in a set time
- a steeplechase section, in which the horse gallops along the course, jumping over ten fences within a set time
- a cross-country section, in which the horse must jump difficult obstacles such as walls, banks and water.

Points are deducted if a rider falls or if the horse fails to complete the course in a set time. At three-day events, the weight of the rider and the saddle must be at least 165 pounds (75 kilograms).

ACTION FACT

Dressage dates back to the time of the ancient Greeks. Soldiers trained their horses to perform movements that would help them evade or attack the enemy during battle.

Jumping tests are part of the three-day event.

EQUESTRIAN
CHAMPIONS

Equestrian sports were first developed by cavalry riders. Early competitions were restricted to army officers.

Today, men and women compete on an equal footing in equestrian competitions. Top riders come from every corner of the globe, but currently most of the top riders come from Europe, the United States and Australia. National and world-class competitions take place around the world. Equestrian events have been a part of the summer Olympics since the Paris Olympics in 1900.

↗ Andrew Hoy

- Born February 8, 1959, Australia
- Has been riding since age 7, when he borrowed a horse from his uncle for his first competition
- Has represented Australia in equestrian events at five Olympic Games, from 1984 to 2000

Career highlights

- Member of Australian team that won a gold medal in the Three-day Event at the Olympic Games in 1992, 1996 and 2000
- Won a silver medal in the Three-day Individual Event at the Sydney Olympics in 2000

↗ Ludger Beerbaum

- Born August 26, 1963, Germany
- Learned to ride on a donkey
- Won his first equestrian competition at age 15

Career highlights

- Won a gold medal in the Individual Jumping competition at the Barcelona Olympics in 1992
- Member of the German Jumping team that won a gold medal at the Olympic Games in 1996 and 2000
- Ranked number one Jumping rider in 2001

↗ David O'Connor

- Born January 18, 1962, Gaithersburg, Maryland
- Took a three-month cross-country trek at age 11 with his mother to gain experience with horses
- Has competed internationally for the United States since 1986
- Currently resides in The Plains, Virgina, with his wife Karen, who also competes in equestrian events

Career highlights

- Completed a rare "triple" with horse Giltedge by winning medals in 1996 Olympic Games, 1998 World Championship and 1999 Pan American Games
- Won gold medal in individual Three-day Event at the Sydney Olympics in 2000
- Member of U.S. Olympic team that won a silver medal in the Three-day Event in 1996 and a bronze medal in 2000
- First two-time winner of USA Equestrian's Equestrian of the Year in 2000 and 2002

↗ Isabell Werth

- Born July 21, 1969, Germany

Career highlights

- Won a gold medal as a member of the German Dressage team at the Barcelona Olympics in 1992
- Won a gold medal as a member of the World Championship team in 1994 and 1998
- Won a gold medal in the Individual Dressage event and as a member of the German Dressage team at the Atlanta Olympics in 1996
- Won a gold medal as a member of the German Dressage team and a silver medal in the Individual Dressage event at the Sydney Olympics in 2000

1868	1900	1912	1921	1930	1931	1939–45
Royal Dublin Society held the first Horse Show, which included two jumping competitions.	The first equestrian events were held in an Olympic Games, in Paris, France.	A full program of events was prepared by Count Clarence von Rosen for the 1912 Stockholm Olympics. The program has remained the same to this day. The first Olympic horse-riding events were only open to army officers.	The Fédération Equestre Internationale (FEI) was formed.	The first Dressage Championships outside of the Olympic Games was organized in Lucerne, Switzerland.	The first rule book for equestrian, called *Rules for the Nations' Cup*, was published by the FEI.	Only three international competitions were held during World War II: two in New York and one in Rome, Italy.

1912

1946	1953	1957	1974	1978	1991	2002
Equestrian competitions began again after World War II.	The first Jumping World Championships were held in Paris, France. The first Three-day Event Championship was held at Badminton, Great Britain.	The first FEI Women's Championships were held.	Women's Jumping Championships were abolished. Women began to compete in the same events as men.	The first World Cup Final was held in Gothenburg, Sweden.	The FEI developed its Code of Conduct, which set standards for the treatment of the horse.	130 countries were members of the FEI. The FEI now regulates all equestrian events.

1999

RELATED ACTION SPORTS

Vaulting

The international sport of vaulting has riders performing exercises on the bare back of a moving horse. There are vaulting competitions for individual riders, pairs of riders, and teams consisting of eight vaulters and one horse. The upper age limit for team vaulters is 18. There is no upper age limit for individual vaulting competitors. There are two parts to vaulting competition: the first part is the compulsory test where all teams do the same set exercises, and a free test, in which each team does its own exercises.

Reining

Reining is the newest equestrian sport to be organized by the FEI. Reining celebrates the work of the cowboys of the west in the United States. Events are designed to show the athletic ability of horse breeds, such as the Pinto and Appaloosa, performing in a show arena. Riders, wearing western cowboy clothes, must perform one of ten approved patterns, including small slow circles, large fast circles, a 360-degree spin on the spot and exciting sliding stops in which the horse is supposed to balance on its back feet while the front feet continue to move. Horses are tacked in a western-style saddle.

↗ Vaulting is like gymnastics on horseback.

↗ All movements in a reining competition are performed at a canter.

GLOSSARY

bascule the horse's position above a fence during a jump, legs tucked up and back rounded

crop a short whip used in horseback riding

dressage a horse-riding event in which the horse performs a series of movements for which it has been trained

driving a horse-riding event where the horse pulls the driver along in a carriage

endurance a long-distance horse-riding competition

eventing horse trials that include dressage, show-jumping and cross-country events

jumping a horse-riding event where the rider urges the horse to jump over obstacles

pommel the part which sticks out at the front and top of a saddle

reining an event from the western part of the United States in which riders perform patterns from memory to demonstrate a variety of stops, turns and figures at various speeds

reins long straps attached to the bit and held in the rider's hands, used to help the rider control the horse

saddle the seat for the rider on the horse's back

temperament the natural manner in which a horse behaves

vaulting an equestrian event that is like gymnastics on horseback

INDEX